A YEAR WITH POPE FRANCIS

Daily reflections from his writings

Edited by Alberto Rossa, CMF

Paulist Press
New York / Mahwah, NJ

Novalis
Toronto, Canada

The quotations in this book are from the writings of Pope Francis when he was Archbishop of Buenos Aires, Argentina, with a few statements made during his first year as pope.

Artwork by Fr. Cerezo Barredo, CMF
Cover and creative design by Ian Dacayanan

Originally published by Claretian Publications, Macao
P.O. Box 1608 Macao, SAR, China
www.bibleclaret.org

This English edition published by Paulist Press
997 Macarther Boulevard
Mahwah, New Jersey 07430
www.paulistpress.com

ISBN: 978-0-8091-4889-9

Published in Canada by Novalis
Publishing Office
10 Lower Spadina Ave., Suite 400
Toronto, Ontario, Canada
M5V 2Z2
www.novalis.ca

Head Office
4475 Frontenac St.
Montreal, Quebec, Canada
H2H 2S2

ISBN: 978-2-89688-023-2

We acknowledge the financial support of the Government of Canada through the Canada Book Fund for business development activities.

Printed and bound in North America

JANUARY

"Do whatever he tells you."
John 2:5

Jesus

Many have spoken about him; now it is time to let him speak to us. We want to know him not only from what others say about him. To hear Pope Francis speak with *"provocative simplicity"* will help rekindle our hope and passion for God and for the world, especially for those in need.

To understand his background we have selected from all his previous writings some quotations that, as a whole, could give us a glimpse of what we are to expect from him as pope. The selection of his words is organized in the form of a calendar for daily prayer and reflection. They are small *"beads"* of his thought, pedagogically arranged to illumine your days, linking them into a living rosary of the mystery of our faith. Take your portion for each day and spend time to savor every word. Every day has its own flavor, its own rhythm. May you unearth treasures of wisdom from the words of Pope Francis to strengthen you in faith, build you up in hope and bring you closer to God and to our brothers and sisters with an *"open mind and faithful heart."*

Table of Contents

reluctant to be served beyond what is strictly necessary, and his service of others is totally devoid of any sense of superiority.

❖ Evangelical simplicity

His preference for simplicity is another aspect that might run against some rituals, formalities and traditions in the Vatican, like not wearing rich, sophisticated papal regalia, or choosing, as he already did, not to live in the pope's palatial apartments. Without any doubt his simplicity will especially be seen in how he addresses himself to the people, like in the use of direct, down to earth expressions everyone can understand.

❖ Hierarchy of truths and virtues

While Pope Francis clearly feels a serious respect for the traditional teachings of the Church and of the earlier popes, it is equally clear to him that there are central issues and concerns in the Church that take priority over other matters and are non-negotiable,

❖ Option for the poor

His preferential option for the poor is part of his life. As an archbishop he always gave special support to priests living in poor neighborhoods. The poor for Jorge Mario Bergoglio are not simply passive listeners of our well-intentioned speeches or mere recipients of *"development programs,"* intended to free them from their suffering. The option for the poor means all these and much more. It is, above all, listening to them, treating them as people who can think for themselves, who have their own initiatives and projects, and who have the right to express the faith in their own way. They are active and creative *"subjects,"* and not *"objects"* of whatever program or pastoral action we might design on their behalf.

❖ Personal poverty

His personal poverty is not for the sake of publicity. Everyone knows he has always been like that: austere to the point of sacrifice. In his heartfelt choice of a poor life he is quite

❖ Popular religiosity

Most of the people from Argentina express their faith by *"popular religiosity"* which carries an original dynamism that creates its own form of expressions, though not always in accordance with the intentions of the ecclesiastical hierarchy. Pope Francis understands these manifestations of the people's faith as the result of the mysterious and free action of the Spirit. When we were at the gathering of the Latin American bishops in Aparecida (Brazil), he told me one night that what interested him the most was how the final document strongly affirmed and validated such an understanding of popular religiosity. He showed this same conviction in many ways in Buenos Aires, always pointing out that pastoral agents are at the service of people, that no one owns such dynamism throbbing in their lives and that instead of criticism and limitations, one has to accompany the people in their popular religiosity and offer them proper channels.

❖ Deep empathy with people

Whenever Bergoglio says the word *"people,"* his eyes sparkle. He values people as the collective subject who should be at the center of the concerns of the Church and of any power. This is not so small matter when some sectors of the society and the Church consider people as only a mass full of defects that must be restructured according to the norms of the *"wise and prudent."* As a bishop he has always insisted that priests be not only merciful but also adapt themselves to people, not keeping up moral or rigid ecclesiastical practices nor complicating the life of people with norms commanded authoritatively from above. *"We are to give the people what the people need"* is a conviction he repeatedly affirms. His is not an opportunistic populism but an attitude guided by the certainty that the Holy Spirit acts in people by ways and means often difficult to comprehend by those who do not share the lives, worries, concerns and aspirations of the people.

tentials in every human person, in the case of Pope Francis the saying should remain as it is: *"What you see is what you get."* In fact, behind his white garments, Francis is the same person he has always been—Jorge Mario Bergoglio— a down-to-earth and humble Argentine Jesuit called to serve, first as the superior of his order in his native country, then as Archbishop of Buenos Aires, and now as Bishop of Rome, always true to himself and to the call he received.

A close friend and collaborator, Fr. Victor Manuel Hernandez, rector of the Catholic University of Argentina and recently appointed archbishop, wrote soon after Bergoglio's election as pope about the innovations he could bring to the Church. His insights can serve as a good introduction to this collection of Francis' thoughts and public pronouncements, mainly from the time he was Archbishop of Buenos Aires.

Introduction

Since his election as Bishop of Rome, Pope Francis has appeared before the Church and the world daring and challenging. His celebrated, unpredictable gestures speak for themselves, to which no one can remain indifferent, especially those used to the corseted environment of the Vatican. His words speak straight to the hearts of believers and unbelievers alike. They are not the words of a theologian, but the voice of a friend, a fellow traveler, a pastor. His messages are short, simple, demanding yet friendly, delivered with the conviction and the spark of one who speaks to be heard, understood and followed. This sort of *"provocative simplicity"* relates to both the sophisticated intellectuals and the simple folk, the pious and the unmindful.

Even if he himself often challenges the well known popular saying, *"What you see is what you get,"* and changes it into *"what you see is not all there is"* in reference to the hidden po-

❖ Church issues

In recent years a style of Church seems to have developed which is not what Pope Francis, as a man of Vatican II, would promote. It must be clearly said that he has always advocated for a missionary and servant Church, not self-centered but focused on serving people. He embraces old women, kisses the poor, visits anyone, attends to or calls the simple people, gives quality time to those who do not have any power, in short: he always shows a stripped, out-of-herself Church. He never gets tired of asking the priests to be available to people, to be always ready to listen and dialogue, not to be ruthless judges, to go out to the peripheries, to take care of the *"disposables"* of society. That has not always been the choice of some men of the Church.

In order for the Church to advance in the way Pope Francis wants, changes and reforms are needed to at least make the procedures more human and evangelical. I do believe that he can do it, even efficiently. Knowing

like love, equality, justice, fraternity. Without downplaying their importance, other issues are only secondary and should not outweigh or obscure the preaching of the gospel and pastoral care of the people, which reflect the Jesus of the Gospel more directly.

❖ Ecumenical and interreligioius commitment

As Archbishop of Buenos Aires he dedicated considerable quality time to talk with non-Catholics. Once again I want to emphasize that it was not a diplomatic strategy. Last year he spent several days locked up with a group of Protestant pastors, sharing with them a retreat. He also got together with the people at a meeting of Pentecostal groups at Luna Park. He had met with Rabbi Skorka at length, and joyfully conferred on him the doctorate *honoris causa* at the UCA [Catholic University of Argentina] despite the criticism this had brought him. *If this is not an open and dialoguing face of the Church, what is?*

✦ *"Cultural exchanges"* or promoting everything that brings people and groups closer, unites and connects them. He is an enthusiast for the common good and social friendship.

✦ *"Take care of the fragility of people."* He continuously asks this of anyone in authority. Influence or power is not for the acquisition of benefits or worldly glory, but to care for the people, to support and assist the weak. *"Taking care"* is, in general, a word that defines him, which he finds embodied in the figure of Saint Joseph.

✦ *"Allow yourself to be treated with mercy."* He is always inviting people who are filled with guilt and scruples to have a self-forgiving attitude and allow themselves to be embraced by the tenderness of Father God. As Pope Francis' fellow Jesuit Angel Rossi says, *"The most fragile always found in him an unconditional father, I would say, even beyond what is possible. I am sure that this magnanimity in front of human frailty will mark his papacy."*

attacks. He is sure that in the end the good and the truth always triumph. I myself went through situations that made me want to disappear, but he firmly supported me: *"Raise your head and do not allow anyone to take away your dignity."*

✦ *"Existential peripheries."* He often invites pastoral agents not to stay locked up but to reach out to the peripheries where no one goes: "Come out of the caves, leave the sacristies." He calls them to get out of their personal comfort or from the circle of nice people, and to be close to all. That is what Jesus did, spending time with the blind man on the road, the leper, the sinful woman.

✦ *"Apostolic zeal,"* or *"self-giving from the heart because no one changes the world by doing things out of obligation."* Only those stirred by inner fire leave footprints behind. That is why he criticizes the *"spiritual worldliness"* of those who cling to external practices or religious appearances, but lack the inner fire of Spirit.

✦ ***"Pray for me"!*** Shows his awareness of his limitations, of being permanently in need of the help of God and the prayer of others. Thus, the first gesture he did as Pope was to bow deeply to the people, asking for their prayer.

✦ ***"Disposables"*** expresses how society crudely ignores those who are unneeded since they are not in the logic of production and consumerism. Because they do not possess beauty, money, power, or youth, they are thrown as garbage to the basket of oblivion.

✦ ***"Humble yourself"*** so that the Lord may continue to do great things. In his Jesuit formation humility is essential for one's best work not to be in vain. When he was offered the papacy he responded, *"I am a sinner, but I accept."*

✦ ***"Boldness."*** He uses this word to encourage those who are afraid or full of worries. For him a person is never completely lost. He does not give up even in the midst of slander and

his acuity, I am sure it will not be easy to deceive him, who was no stranger to power as an archbishop. He was already showing a way of understanding the exercise of the papacy, from a good theological point of view, when he presented himself from the first moment, and insistently, as bishop of Rome. He is Pope in as much as he is Bishop of Rome, a local church, which indicates an exercise of power markedly decentralized, that respects procedures, options, decisions, local histories and culture.

TYPICAL EXPRESSIONS

Here are some expressions Pope Francis frequently uses:

✦ *"Self-referential"* indicates a church that is navel-gazing, locked up in intrigues, internal or worldly needs rather than being open and surrendering with joy and in humble service to the people.

The center is Jesus, not the successor of Peter.

It is there in the wounds
of Jesus that we are truly secure;
there we encounter
the boundless love of his heart.
I have seen so many people
who find the courage
to enter the wounds of Jesus
by saying to him,
"Lord, I am here, accept my poverty,
hide my sin in your wounds
and wash it away with your blood."
And I always see
that God does just this:
He welcomes, consoles,
cleanses and loves.

❧ In order to solve
their problems,
many people resort to
fortunetellers and tarot cards.
*But only Jesus saves
and we must bear witness to this!*
He is the only one.

Encountering Jesus always
entails a call, great or small,
but always a call
(cf. Mt 4:19; 9:9; 10:1-4).
This call happens at any time
and is pure gratuitousness
(Mt 20:5-6),
but an encounter that has
to be sought out
(cf. Mt 8:2-3; 9:9),
sometimes with heroic constancy
(cf. Mt 15:21ff)
or clamor
(cf. Mt 8:25),
and the search is not free
from confusion and doubt
(cf. Lk 7:18-24; Mt 11:2-7).

❧ Welcome the Risen Christ
into your life
as a friend,
with trust:
He is Life!

Christians should be
the first *(and often we are not!)*
in rejecting the hasty identification
of maturity with adaptation.
Jesus, no less,
was considered by many people
of his time the paradigm
of the maladjusted
and, therefore,
the immature.

Jesus
power of God's love
conquered
and defeated
it with his resurrection.

❧ Ours is a joy
that comes not from
having many possessions
but from having met
a person, Jesus,
who has a message for us: mercy.
Let us ask for the grace
not to get tired of asking
for forgiveness
because he never gets tired
of forgiving.

🐦 Young people,
you must say to the world:

"To follow Christ *is good,*
love Christ *is good,*
the message of Christ *is good,*
announce Him to the ends
of the earth is good!"

We are like the Apostles
in the Gospel:
often we prefer
to hold on to our security,
to stand in front of a tomb,
to think about someone
who has died,
someone who ultimately lives
only as a memory
like the great historical figures
from the past.
We are afraid of God's surprises!
He always surprises us!
Jesus is the everlasting
today of God.

> ✒ Our daily
problems and worries
can lead us
to sadness and bitterness...
and that's where death is.
*That is not the place
to look for the One
who is alive!*

Jesus | 31

If till now
you have kept Jesus at a distance,
go near him.
He will receive you
with open arms.
If you have been indifferent,
dare to risk
and you won't be disappointed.
If following him seems difficult,
don't be afraid, but trust him
and be confident that he is
close to you, he is with you.
He will give you the peace
you are looking for
and the strength
to live as he would have you do.

Openness to others
reflects our openness to the Lord.
It is he, the one with an open heart,
the only one who can open a space
for peace in our hearts,
that peace which makes us
open to others.

Jesus 33

We, Christians,
may do as much as we want,
but if we do not
confess Jesus Christ,
we become simply an NGO,
not the Church,
not the Bride of Christ.

Today Jesus might,
at first glance,
appear to be boring
and not so exciting,
but in him are hidden
all the treasures of wisdom
and charity,
all the richness of love,
faith and hope.

In the today of Jesus,
there is no room
for fear
or uncertainty
or anguish
or conflicts
because in the Lord's today
"love overcomes
fear and uncertainty,
anguish and conflicts."

There is no place
for anguish
because today is in the hands
of the Father,
who *"knows very well
what we need"*
and in his hands
we feel that
*"each day has enough
trouble of its own."*

Jesus | 37

❧ Quite often in our life
tears are the glasses
through which to see Jesus.
One can weep for many reasons:
out of goodness,
for our sins,
for graces received,
out of joy like Mary Magdalene.
Let us ask the Lord for the
beautiful grace of tears
to prepare ourselves to see him.

When we are called
by the Lord,
we find that the call
is quite heavy to carry.
We feel afraid,
and in some cases,
a fear bordering on panic.
Relax!
It is only the beginning of a cross
which also carries with it
an irresistible attraction
to the Lord who,
by the same calling,
seduces us with
a blazing fire to follow him
(cf. Jer 20:7-18).

Jesus | 39

How does God console?
Certainly not with
pious platitudes like,
*"after all the tribulation
it's not as bad as it seems."*
On the contrary,
he allows us to see the suffering
that has befallen us in all its horrors,
but silently and calmly
he shows us heaven.

In the greatest abandonment
on the cross,
Jesus pronounces
the word *"Father"*
with human tenderness
carried to the limit,
and with that same tenderness
he pronounces
it also in heaven.

The resurrection
of Jesus Christ is not
the happy ending of a movie.
It is the intervention of God
against and above any human hope,
as it proclaims as *"Lord"*
the one who accepted
the path of defeat so that
the power of the Father
may be revealed and glorified.

The love Jesus proposes is free and unlimited, and that's why many consider his teaching unreasonable and crazy, preferring instead to go along the trodden path of mediocrity.

Look around you.
How many wounds do our
personal sins inflict on humanity:
wars and violence, the thirst for money,
power, corruption, and crimes against
human life and creation?
In short, it all is our failure to love
and respect God and our neighbor.
But let us look even more intently
at Jesus on the cross, assuming and
carrying upon his shoulders
all the sins and failures
of humankind and, with the strength
of the love of God,
conquering and defeating them
all with his resurrection.

❧ Dear friends,
with Christ everyone can
overcome the evil
that is in us and in the world.
Don't believe the evil one,
who tells us,
*"You cannot do anything
against violence, corruption,
injustice, against your sins.
That's the way it is
and you better get used to it."*
Wrong! With Christ we can
transform ourselves and the world
by bringing about the victory
of the cross of Christ,
the sign of the great love of God
to all and everywhere.

Jesus | 45

The resurrection of Christ
is our greatest assurance,
our most precious treasure.
*How can we not share
this treasure
and beautiful assurance
with others?*

Mary

Look once
and a thousand times
to the Virgin Mary.
*May she intercede with her Son
for the appropriate gesture
and word which will
allow us to announce
the Good News to everyone,
keeping always in mind
that the Church does not grow
by proselytizing
but by inviting
and welcoming!*

❋ The *"yes"* of Nazareth
given by Mary
in faith turns into charity.
She who by the work
of the Holy Spirit
was made the mother of the Son,
being moved by that same Spirit,
was transformed into a servant
of all for love of her Son.

❧ The mystery of the Church
is very much linked
to the mystery of Mary,
the mother of God
and mother of the Church.
Mary bears and cares for us,
so does the Church;
and like Mary,
the Church makes us grow.

FEBRUARY

"Jesus said:
*You will be my true disciples
if you keep my word.*"
John 8:31

Discipleship

To collectively create
a better reality within the limits
and possibilities of history
is an act of hope.
It is not a matter of certainties
or mere bets, neither of fate
nor of chance.
It demands beliefs and virtues.
It is to put into play
all the resources,
plus an imponderable *"extra"*
that gives it drama.

꙰ The Christian paradox
requires that the itinerary
of the heart of the disciple
is to leave in order to remain,
to change in order to be faithful.
Our task is to start living in full
but in another way,
by becoming witnesses and builders
of another way of being human.
By implementing
our deepest conviction
not only can things be changed
but we also realize
that *"we need
and can change them."*

Discipleship | 53

❧ We, Christians, believe
that not everything is the same;
that we are not alone in the universe
or aimlessly wondering
in it without purpose.
And this, which at first glance may
seem so *"spiritual,"*
can also be quite decisive
and lead to a radical shift
in our way of life,
in the projects that we imagine
and try to develop, in the certainties
and values we hold and transmit.

⌀ The Church was, is
and will always be persecuted.
The Church will be persecuted
not precisely in the mediocre children
who pact with the world as those
renegades referred to by the book of
Maccabees (cf. 1 Macc 1:11-15)
who are never persecuted,
but in those other children who,
amid the cloud of so many witnesses,
opt to have their eyes fixed on Jesus
(cf. Heb 12:1-2) and follow in his steps
whatever the price may be.

When what is sought
is the *"truth,"*
the *"good"* is also necessary.
Both are always together,
enhancing each other.
The truth is not intended
to split, attack,
disqualify,
and disintegrate.

The apostle
does not belong
to himself/herself,
but is buried with Christ
(Col 2:12).
Any other way
is to be ashamed of Christ
and, therefore, to face
the eschatological consequences:
*"If anyone is ashamed of me
and of my words in this adulterous
and sinful generation,
also the Son of Man will be ashamed
of him when he comes in the glory
of his Father with his holy angels"*
(Mk 8:38).

❧ Following Jesus
leads the disciples
to carry their own cross
for the love of their Lord.
An apostolic zeal understood
as a *"business"* does not recognize
the saving dimension
of walking along the same path
of torment and crucifixion
that Jesus walked,
which could only be inflicted on those
who were not Roman citizens....
The disciple has to be prepared
to be taken as a *"Roman criminal"*
and face the consequences as He did.

Society

All utopias include
not only a description
of an ideal society
but also an analysis
of the mechanisms or strategies
that could make the utopia possible.
We could say that
it is a projection into the future
that tends to return to the present
to take a vividly outlined shape and,
then looks for the right mediations
to make it a reality.

❧ There is nothing worse
than a Christian educational
institution conceived from uniformity
and standard expected behavior…
*Our goal is not only to form
"individuals useful to society,"
but also to educate people
who can transform it!*
This cannot be achieved
by sacrificing the skills
that lead to maturity,
the deepening of knowledge,
diversification of tastes because,
finally, to neglect those *"results"*
will produce not *"new men and
women"* but lifeless puppets
of a consumerist society.

☞ A society that tends
to turn people into puppets
of production and consumption
always opts for results.
It needs control;
it cannot give rise to novelty
without seriously compromising
its purposes and without
increasing the degree
of already existing conflict.
It prefers that the other
be completely predictable
in order to acquire
the maximum profit
with a minimum of expenditure.

It is anti-human
to privatize social
development and welfare.
Regarding this,
the state has to assume
the role of encourager,
integrator,
responsible auditor,
but must not decline
the responsibility proper
to its nature:
to care for the common good
of the people.

Let's open our eyes,
the slave is not one who is chained,
but the one who does not think
nor has convictions.
You are a citizen
not by the mere act of voting,
but by your vocation
and commitment
to build a nation of solidarity.

Capitalism tends
to tame religion to prevent
it from being too bothersome.
It fosters a civilization
of consumerism,
hedonism, political deals
between the political powers
and the kingdom of money.

The structures of this world
are not only and exclusively sinful.
To affirm the contrary is dualism.
The wheat and weeds
grow together and,
as parents,
our humble mission
is to protect the wheat,
leaving the mowing
of the weeds
to the angels.

❧ The memory of people
is not a computer
but a heart.
People,
like Mary,
keep things
in their hearts.

❧ Mere intentions or words
are not enough.
They should be put
to work effectively.
It is nice to talk about solidarity,
of a different society,
theorizing about the importance
of schools and of an updated,
personalized,
down-to-earth education.
There are millions of words
circulating in the information
society in which knowledge
is the primary capital.
But *"with good intentions
the road to hell is paved."*

✐ True creativity
does not forsake purposes,
values, meaning.
But at the same time
it does not ignore
the specific aspects
of project implementation.
Competence without ethics
is empty and dehumanizing,
like the blind leading the blind,
but the application of the ends
without adequate consideration
of the means to achieve them
is doomed to become
mere fantasy.

❧ Utopia can turn into *"madness,"* of *"alienation"* when it does not develop mediations to make its visions attractive and possible.

When there is no
social solidarity,
the elderly are simply abandoned,
and not just amid material insecurity.
They are abandoned
when we don't accept
their limitations,
reflected in the many pitfalls
they must overcome to survive
in a civilization which does not
allow them to participate,
to give an opinion or be taken
into account in the consumerist model
that proclaims *"only the youth
are to be taken seriously
and allowed to enjoy
all human rights."*

❧ Economic liberalism
leaves the poor people
for the trash can.

🌿 In our cities
there are people
who perform human sacrifices
by killing the dignity
of men and women,
girls and boys,
who are subjected to slavery
for economic or shameful reasons.
We cannot remain idle!

This culture applies
the *"death penalty"* through
abortion and hidden euthanasia
of the elderly through
neglect and maltreatment…
when, in fact, the elderly are the seat
of wisdom of the people.
Children are maltreated as well
when they are neither educated
nor adequately nourished.
Many young boys and girls
are forced to prostitute themselves
and be exploited.

It is clear
though some may insist
otherwise even today
that a model of rigid historical,
national identities
with no room left
for dissenter for different options
and visions cannot take place
anymore, at least
in our Western societies.

The respect
for the human person
in our modern culture,
despite their inconsistencies
and abuses, is already
an achievement of humanity.
This development of the concept
of the human person
as subject of an inviolable
freedom and dignity
has not been possible
without evangelical inspiration.

It is unfortunate that we live
in a time where the elderly
are not valued and are
put to one side because
they are considered a nuisance.
However, old people are those
who tell us the history of things,
who carry forward the faith
and give it to us to inherit.
Open your minds and hearts
to the all-embracing,
increasing diversity which is
becoming more and more
the social characteristic of our times

Society | 77

❧ When society is organized
in such a way that not everyone
has the opportunity to work...
then there is something
wrong with that society.
It is not right!
It goes against God.

❧ Let us never forget
that authentic power
is service.

The exercise
of seeking
cumulative power
as adrenaline
is artificial fullness today
and self-destruction tomorrow.

❧ Power
as unique ideology
is another lie.

MARCH

*"The word of God
is living and effective,
sharper than any two-edged sword."*
Hebrews 4:12

We never know
quite for sure
when we are actually
reaching people
with our actions.
We don't know it,
for better or worse,
until those actions
have produced their effects,
and produce effects
they will.

There is the true,
the beautiful,
the good and,
of course,
the absolute.
They constitute
the permanent pillars
of education.
They should be pointed to,
perceived,
known and lived.

❧ Education
must overcome the risk
of downgrading itself
by being a mere distribution
of knowledge.
It is not only the selection
of contents or methods
but also of interpretation
and assessment.

❧ While we see all kinds
of intolerance and fundamentalism
taking over relations
between individuals, groups
and peoples, let's dare to live
and teach the value of respect
and love beyond all differences.

🐦 Christian victory
is always a cross,
but a cross
that is a flag
of victory.

🖎 Impatience
carries within itself
a punishment: sterility.
The impatient,
by wanting it all at once,
is left with nothing.
Their projects are like the seed
that fell on rocky soil:
they lack depth;
they are mere words
without consistency.

🍂 There are many vanities
seeping into us,
but the most common
is defeatism.

In a society where lies, concealment and hypocrisy erode the basic trust that makes basic social bonds possible, *what innovation can be more revolutionary other than the truth?*
We must, therefore, speak and tell the truth that exposes our criteria, our values, our views.
If we ourselves refuse to say any lie at all, we also as an overflowing effect will become more responsible and even more charitable.
Lying dilutes everything and really shows what is in our hearts.

🌮 Always speak
the truth
in our schools.
I assure you,
something new
will happen.

🐚 Listening,
acceptance of failures and mistakes,
admission of errors,
in short, assuming our weakness,
are indeed the necessary ingredients
for a dialogue in search
of the truth leading us all
to build a common project.

 Each of us has a
vision of good and of evil.
We have to encourage people
to move towards what they
think is Good. That would
be enough to make the
world a better place.

🖋 We must restore hope
to young people,
help the old,
be open to the future,
spread love. Be poor
among the poor.
We need to include the
excluded and preach peace.

🐚 People cannot simply
"be counted"
or *"be a number."*
In relation to each other
and to the world,
the human person
can never be reduced
to just another statistic.

Christian Values

🖎 To give priority
to the values of the mind
over the values of the heart
is a great temptation,
which is wrong.
Only the heart unites and integrates.
Understanding without empathy
and feelings tends to divide.
The heart unites
the idea with reality,
time with space
and life with death and eternity.

❧ We need to bless
the present,
speak well of others
as we look for
what builds up and unites;
we need to talk about
the beautiful things we share
and go beyond
different perspectives
for the common good.

🌮 Granted,
efficiency is a value in itself
but as the ultimate criterion,
forget it!

🕊 Let it be said
without irreverence:
there is no one more inefficient
than God.
Consider the lack of logic
in His investment and
in the purpose of that spending:
sacrificing his Son for a sinful
and ungrateful humanity,
past and present.
There is no doubt,
the logic of the history of salvation
is a gratuitous logic
not measured by
a *"must"* and a *"should."*

🐦 *Why don't we try to live*
and transmit the priority
of non-quantifiable values: friendship,
the ability to simply celebrate
the good moments of life,
sincerity that encourages peace,
confidence and trust?
It may be easy to say,
as poetic as these values may sound,
but extremely demanding
to live them, since it requires
that we stop worshiping the god
of *"efficiency-at-all-cost"*,
so deeply rooted in
our post-modern mindset.

🖋 There is not much difference
between those who closed
their doors to Joseph and Mary
because they were poor outsiders
and Herod who killed the children
because fear had killed his heart.
There is no middle way
between light and darkness,
pride and humility, truth and lie.
Either we open the door to Jesus,
who comes to save us,
or we close ourselves
in the sufficiency and pride
of self-deliverance.

Christian Values | 101

❧ To approach others
in the right ways
means to communicate
the beauty of charity in truth.
When the truth
is painful and difficult
to express,
beauty lies
in that love which shares
the pain with respect
and in a dignified manner.

It is not possible
to build bridges
between people
while forgetting God.
The Catholic Church
is aware of the importance
of the promotion of friendship
and respect between men and women
of different religious traditions.
I wish to repeat this:
the promotion of friendship
and respect between men and women
of different religious traditions.

Christian Values

🖎 The pastoral work
of our parishes
should involve reflection,
logistics, planning, etc.,
but only in order to dedicate
more quality time
to the important task:
works of charity.

🐚 Vigilant prayer
is the wisdom
to discern,
recognize
and hold God
as He passes
by our side
(Mk 6:48; Lk 24:28).

Witness

❧ God
does not want
a house built
on stone
but on faithfulness
to his word
and to his plan.

❁ Let us break
open our heart
and believe in the gospel,
not in the fake gospel,
not in the light gospel,
not in the watershed gospel
but in the gospel of truth.

The experience
of the beautiful love of God
in a personal and communal
encounter with Jesus Christ
is the engine
of Christian creativity
for the announcement
of the Good News.

🌿 If you want
to be faithful
and fruitful,
our homilies
should always
disseminate
and harvest hope.

❧ To embark on following
Jesus Christ,
courage is needed;
that courage which
only comes from God
gives us the apostolic
endurance and strength
to bear abuses, insults,
and all kind of hardships
in preaching
the gospel.

Witness

The Church will be
persecuted in the measure
of her fidelity to the gospel.
The testimony to this fidelity
bothers and enrages the world,
making it kill and destroy,
as it happened
in the case of Stephen,
the first among the disciples
to shed his life for Christ.

The word of God is creative;
and the Word he said,
once and for all,
to human beings couldn't be other
but the Word made flesh,
his Son, Jesus Christ.
However only those
who hear the Word made flesh
from their experience of personal
sinfulness and weakness
will receive his saving power.
This is the reason why the Lord says
he has come for the sick,
not the healthy.

❧ This is the way
our Church wants us to be today:
men and women free
of compromises,
unprejudiced,
free of ambitions,
and free from ideologies,
in other words,
men and women
of the gospel
and only the gospel.

Humility

~ *"Triumphalism"*
is a great temptation
for Christians.
Even the Apostles fell into it.
The Lord teaches with his life
and death that there should not be
a place for triumphalism
among his followers.

~ When the Lord looks
at our fragility, he invites us
to take care of it not with
fear but with courage.
*"Don't be afraid,
I have overcome the world"!*
(Jn 16:33).
*"I am with you always
until the end of the world"*
(Mt 28:20).
Therefore, the awareness
of one's own fragility and
its acknowledgment, will not make
the Lord withdraw from us, but, on
the contrary, will move him as in the
case of Peter to send us on a mission,
to urge us to set out into the
deep water and become
fishers of people.

Humility | 117

Those who seek the truth
become humble persons
for they know that truth
is difficult to be found,
and much more so when
one searches in solitude.
The truth is to be searched for
and found with others.
Falsifying the truth insulates,
separates, divides us; on the contrary,
looking for it unites, brings us closer,
makes us encounter each other and,
when found, fills us with joy,
making us better
brothers and sisters.

~ *"It is a must"* for
the young religious to be able,
when necessary,
to accuse themselves.
It sometimes requires an uncommon
amount of courage because
it is like opening our inner doors
to others, allowing them
to see beyond our appearances,
without any pretense.
Then, the truth is revealed
and we are justified
by the Lord in our humility.

Humility | 119

To accuse ourselves
is to assume the role of culprit
as the Lord did
when he took upon his shoulders
our faults and failures.
The one who accuses himself
leaves room for
the mercy of God,
like the publican of the Gospel
who dared not lift up
his eyes from the ground.

～ Our evangelizing vocation
asks us to cultivate the humility
of being stewards, not masters,
who assume the reproach
and contempt for
the cross of Christ
in our daily work,
in the service
of the Son of God
who went before us
along the way.

Humility | 121

～ The more we are aware
of our exalted
vocation and mission,
the more we feel the human
limitation of our own flesh.
Abraham, our father in faith,
experienced it when,
overwhelmed by the promises
of the Lord, he humbly confessed:
*"I don't have children
and a servant
will inherit what is mine"*
(Gen 15:2-3).

Jesus enters Jerusalem
to die on the cross,
and it is precisely here
where his condition as king
according to God shines.
The cross became
his royal throne.

Suffering

❧ When we journey
without the cross,
when we build without the cross,
when we profess Christ
without the cross,
we are not disciples of the Lord,
we are worldly;
we may be bishops, priests,
cardinals, popes,
but not disciples
of the Lord.

❧ The age of martyrs
is not yet over,
even today we can say,
in truth, that the Church
has more martyrs
now than during
the first centuries.

Suffering

❧ *What kind of a King is Jesus?*
Let us take a look at him:
he rides on a donkey;
he is not accompanied
by a court nor surrounded
by an army as a symbol of power.
Jesus does not enter the Holy City
to receive honors but a
crown of thorns, a staff
and a purple robe. His kingship
becomes an object of derision.
He enters to go up to Calvary,
carrying his burden of wood
in order to die on the cross.
And it is precisely here
that his kingship shines
forth in godly fashion:
his royal throne
is the wood of the cross!

Suffering | 127

❧ One word should suffice,
that is, the cross itself.
The cross is the word
through which God has responded
to evil in the world.
Sometimes it may seem
as though God does not
react to evil, as if he is silent.
And yet, God has spoken,
he has replied, and his answer
is the cross of Christ:
a word that is love,
mercy and forgiveness.
It also reveals a judgment,
namely that God,
in judging us, loves us.

❧ Christ's cross
embraced with love
never leads to sadness
but to the joy
of having been saved
and of doing a little
of what he did for us.

*❧ Dear young people:
with Christ the heart
never grows old!
Do not be ashamed
of his cross!
On the contrary,
embrace it
because it is in giving
ourselves to others
that we have true joy.*

❧ Cowardice
is to throw the towel
at the first challenge;
It is like descending
from the cross to fight
our own battle,
not that of the Lord.

❧ To embrace the cross,
courage and endurance are needed.
There are some *"strong"* Christians
who undertake apostolic work
but falter when
faced with difficulty.
They don't know
about patience.

❧ Those who share
in the cross do not need
to verify their activity
with triumphalism
because they know
that the cross itself
is already
a triumphant victory.

❧ To the generosity of Christ
one cannot respond
with a conventional
and polite *"thank you"*;
one has to give his/her life
in order to follow him.

❧ The cross marks
the *"militant dimension"*
of our existence.
With the cross
one cannot negotiate
or dialogue or bargain;
either one embraces it
or rejects it.

Suffering | 135

❧ The Lord has shaken you;
he has done it without anesthesia,
like he did to Abraham,
asking him to give up his son,
his dreams, his projects.
He tested him without explanation,
introducing him to the school
of detachment to be truly a free man
and completely available
to the projects of God
who was planning
to make him a collaborator
in the great history of salvation.

❧ According to the gospel
the way to reach out
to our suffering brothers
and sisters is to open one's heart,
to be moved,
to touch their sores
and carry the wounded.
It is also to pay the two *"denari"*
and, finally, to be the guarantor
for whatever more would be spent.
We will be judged by this.

❦ The exquisite elites
know how to pucker their noses
when confronted with failure;
they are scandalized.
They prefer to set up models
of the Church based
on *"common sense"*
rather than on the failure
of the cross.

❧ It is in the cross
that Jesus clearly takes on failure
and evil and transcends them.
There, his unfathomable love
is manifested because
only the one who loves
that much has the freedom
and the fortitude of spirit
to accept failure.
Jesus died as a loser.

❧ In his death,
Jesus assumed
and gave meaning
to all the failures
in the history of salvation.
Only one solution remains:
the divine solution,
the resurrection
as revolutionary ferment.

Life

🦋 Typical of the clergy's apathy
is the failure to take care
of people who are part of
our pastoral action.
We see that many
are tempted by apathy.
It brings disintegration because
it is life that integrates and apathy
is a subtle negation of life.

🌿 Over the years
the character of certain people,
turns sour like bad wine.
To be a cheerful elderly person
whose advice is respectfully sought
for by his/her children
or to be a grandparent whose
grandchildren visit with joy
in order to listen to his/her stories
does not simply happen.
Nor does becoming an old crafty,
nagging, unapproachable, immature
geezer simply happen just like that.
The preparation for what we will be
as senior citizens begins now
by simply being gentle,
tolerant and kind.

🌸 The loss of the initial fervor
leads some middle age people
to a kind of fervent rushing to what
we might call *"secondary tasks"*
or *"secondary virtues."*
Some are driven to the social sphere
with a commitment that separates them
from the conventional liturgical forms.
Others instead become
keepers of fanatic rites.
Midlife crisis is an invitation
from the Lord to deepen
one's theological virtues,
which lead *"to focus only
on Jesus Christ."*

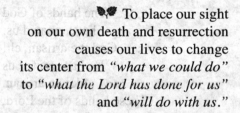

To place our sight
on our own death and resurrection
causes our lives to change
its center from *"what we could do"*
to *"what the Lord has done for us"*
and *"will do with us."*

The hands of God
have created us:
God the artisan, eh!
He has created us
like an artisan.
These hands of the Lord,
the hands of God, have
not abandoned us.

The hands of God are blistered with love and accompany us on the path of life. Let us entrust ourselves to the hands of God, like a child entrusts himself to the hand of his father. This is a safe hand!"

MAY

"Whatever you do to the least of my brothers or sisters you do to me."

Matthew 25:40

Solidarity

To overcome
the destructive ethics
of competition of all against all,
one has to carry out a practice
of solidarity, destroying the roots
of selfishness in an effective way,
not remaining in mere
proclamations and complaints
but placing our best capabilities
at the service of this ideal.
High end and adequate means:
the excellence of solidarity.

Solidarity

Solidarity,
rather than an individual
or affective attitude,
is a way of understanding
and living our task
in the human society.
It is in fact
the *"certificate of authenticity"*
of the Christian life.

Education for solidarity
is not only about teaching to be good
and generous or raising funds,
participating in social work,
and supporting foundations.
It is also about creating a new
mentality, thinking in terms
of community, prioritizing
everyone's life and well-being
above greediness and egoism.

Solidarity | 151

 Our schools must follow
a well-defined criterion:
that of solidarity which, allow me
to say, should indelibly mark
the educational endeavor of Christian
teachers in as much as they,
above and beyond any other jobs,
are dealing with persons,
the little ones, who are put under
their care to help them
become fully human.
The criterion that breaks
the logic of competitive
individualism is solidarity.

Solidarity

◈ We know that our young people
have a huge capacity to feel
the suffering of others and engage
in actions of solidarity.
This social sensitivity,
often just emotional,
should nevertheless be educated
to become a solidarity which
reflexively discovers and unmasks
the link between obviously painful
and unjust situations and
the ideologies and practices
that produce or reproduce them.

Solidarity | 153

The only way to counteract
the pervasive consumerism
and competitive individualism
presently undermining the life
of our people is to reconstruct
the values of a solidarity
and sense of community
from the experience
of authentic human encounters,
illuminated by the gospel.

Only the one who recognizes
his/her own vulnerability
is capable of practicing solidarity.
To be affected by those who are
out or at the edge of the road
and to sympathize
with them is the attitude
of the men and women
who recognize their own faces,
both muddy and precious,
in the faces of others
and, therefore,
do not reject them.

Solidarity

To believe that every person
is my brother or sister
is the condition that makes
our own humanity possible,
therefore, everything we do
(and I stress: everything)
should ultimately be focused
on how to find, discover,
perfect and disseminate
concrete ways of knowing
and living this fundamental truth.

To be truly neighbors
means to consider love
as our main task.
Let us, therefore,
dare to recover
the liberating potential
of this Christian
commandment of love,
which is capable of creating
a true democratic coexistence
by injecting it with
real and lived communion,
open to inclusiveness,
listening, dialoguing,
respecting other's opinions
and orientations.

Solidarity | 157

A *"happy life"*
is not such without including
my fellow men and women,
like there is not a true
and effective humanism
that does not proclaim *"love"*
as the vital link between
human beings
at every possible level:
intimate, interpersonal,
social, religious,
political, intellectual, etc.

❰❱ The Lord
has no verbal excesses
or flamboyant gestures
in the Gospel,
except with his hands
which are always blessing,
healing, sharing, caressing,
washing feet
and touching wounds.
Jesus wants to be
all-powerful
by breaking bread
with his hands.

Solidarity | 159

To *"see"* the people
and realize that they *"exist"*
is not enough to help them.
First, we must listen as they tell us
about themselves, their needs,
desires, joys, and sufferings.
Appearances are often deceiving.
Listening is a great grace.
Simply said, listening is not
just hearing, it is being attentive,
willing to understand, value,
respect, in short to place
ourselves in their shoes.

Solidarity

Here is the *"Good News"*
of Jesus about human dignity:
"God so loved the world that He gave
his only son, so that everyone
who believes in him may not perish
but may have eternal life.
Indeed, God did not send the Son
into the world to condemn the world,
but in order that the world might
be saved through him"
(Jn 3:16-17).
Only the one who recognizes
the infinite dignity of the *"other"*
is capable of giving up
one's life for her/him.

Solidarity | 161

There is a truly evangelical
principle that serves as foolproof
to unmask the excluding
the only-one-way ideologies
and false utopias that close
the possibility of hope;
it is the criterion of universality:
*"the whole human being
and all human beings"*
which Pope Paul VI proposed
as the criteria for
every true development.

And now let us begin
this journey of the Bishop
of Rome and his people;
that is, the journey of the Church
of Rome which presides
in charity over all the Churches;
a journey of love
and mutual trust.
Let us always pray
for one another and
for the whole world
that there might be a great sense
of brother/sisterhood.

Solidarity | 163

Work

🙠 Some time back
I was telling you:
come out of the caves!
Today I repeat:
come out of the sacristy,
of the parish's offices,
of the VIP rooms!
Get out!
Engage in the pastoral
of the atrium,
of the doors,
of the houses,
of the street.
Don't wait;
get out!

No deprivation can be worse than not being able to earn one's bread, than being denied the dignity of work.

Those operating a business
in a country and then taking
the profit abroad to place it
in fiscal paradises for instance,
commit a sin by not honoring
the country making possible
their wealth or the people
who worked to generate it.

Not paying a just wage
or not providing work,
focusing exclusively
on the balance sheets,
financial statements
or personal profit…
all this goes against God.

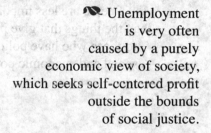

Unemployment
is very often
caused by a purely
economic view of society,
which seeks self-centered profit
outside the bounds
of social justice.

🙾 People are less important than the things that give profit to those who have political, social and economic power.

❧ God entrusts man and woman
with the task of filling
the earth and subduing it.
It does not mean exploiting it,
but nurturing and protecting it,
caring for it by their work.
Work is part of God's loving plan;
we are called to cultivate
and care for all the goods of the earth,
thus participating
in the work of creation.

❧ Our task:
to care for everyone,
for each one, with love,
especially for the children,
the elderly, those who are more
fragile and often remain
on the periphery of our heart.
The family is to worry about
one another; the spouses caring
for each other and for their children,
and also the children
becoming caregivers
to their parents.

Creativity

❧ One who breaks ground
cannot remain without scars
on the body and soul.

🦋 Being creative is not throwing
away all that constitute the current
reality however limited, corrupt
and worn out it presents itself.
There is no future without
a present and without a past.
Creativity, in other words,
means memory and insight,
fairness and justice,
wisdom and strength.

The strength of change
comes directly from our faith in the
Risen Christ, the ultimate novelty
that declares all other realizations
provisional and incomplete,
a novelty that measures the distance
between the actual
and the manifestation of
a new heaven and a new earth.

❧ It is not enough to be
"generous" and *"good."*
It is not enough for our neediest
brothers and sisters, victims
of injustice and exclusion,
for whom the best intentions
are of little or no help in their needs.
It is not even good for our own selves
such useless solidarity which only
serves to slightly alleviate the
feelings of guilt. The need is for
higher targets and adequate means.
In our apostolic boldness
we need to be intelligent, capable,
efficient, and all these involve effort,
and search, creativity, and
deep commitment!

Creativity

❦ The creativity that thrives
on utopia is rooted in solidarity
and seeks for the most effective ways,
but it may suffer, nonetheless,
from a disease that corrupts it into
the worst of evils: to believe that
it all starts with us, an attitude
which quickly degenerates
into authoritarian imposition
or brutal replacement of one *"truth"*
for another, *"my truth."*
Only God creates out of nothing.
Our creativity should bring out
the *"new"* in continuity from
the valuable elements we already have,
just as there is no way to cure
a sick person without relying
on other healthy parts of the body.

Freedom

Our freedom becomes
fully mature when it is a responsible
freedom, that is, when it becomes
the meeting place of
the *"three dimensions of time."*
When we recognize what we did
or failed to do *(the past leading to the
present)*; when we measure, ponder
and assume the consequences
(the present) and, thus prepared,
act now and make decisions
(the present leading to the future).
That is mature freedom.

🖎 Freedom is not an end in itself,
like a black hole behind
which there is nothing.
Freedom must be governed by love,
by the unconditional affirmation
of life and, therefore,
the value of all and each one of us.
Freedom is ordered
to the fuller life of the person,
of everybody, of all men
and women.

🕮 We already know the saying,
*"Your freedom ends where
the freedom of others begins."*
As a consequence
*"if others cease to exist,
you would be freer."*
This is the exaltation of the individual
"against" others, the legacy of Cain:
if it belongs to him,
it is not mine;
if it is mine,
it cannot belong to any other.

JUNE

"Every high priest is taken among mortals, and appointed, to be their representative before God."
Hebrews 5:1

Church

✍ When the Church
does not empower the laity,
she is no longer a mother
but a babysitter who puts
the baby to sleep.
She is a dormant Church.

If I had to choose between
a wounded Church
that goes out onto the streets
and a sick withdrawn Church,
I would definitcly choose the first.
Between a rugged Church
coming out to the streets
and a Church sick of self-referential
narcissism, without doubt,
I prefer the first.
When the Church does not walk,
she falls apart like a sandcastle.

Instead of just being a Church which welcomes and receives, we should be a Church that goes out of itself to the men and women who do not participate in parish life, ignore or do not care about it. We should organize missions in public squares where people usually gather and, then, pray, celebrate Mass, offer baptism to be administered after an adequate preparation.

A good priest can be recognized
by the way his people are anointed.
This is a clear test.
When our people are anointed
with the oil of gladness
as they leave the church
after the Mass, they will look
very much like people
who have heard
the good news.

Church | 187

🐾 Be shepherds
who live with
"the smell of the sheep,"
shepherds in the midst
of their flock,
fishers of people.

⊱❧ We need to avoid
the spiritual sickness of a Church
wrapped up in her own world.
It is true that going out on
to the streets implies the risk
of accidents happening as it would
be for any ordinary man or woman.

We need to *"go out,"* then, in order to test and experience our own anointing and its power and redemptive efficacy into the *"outskirts"* where there is suffering, bloodshed, blindness longing for sight and prisoners under so many evil masters.

    Ⅎ We should not simply
remain in our own secure world,
that of the ninety-nine sheep
who never strayed from the fold,
but we should go out with Christ
in search of the one lost sheep,
however far it may
have wandered.

ぐ**ゞ** If the Church stays
"indoors," she certainly will age.
The Church is called to come out
of herself and to go to
the *"existential peripheries,"*
where the mystery of sin, pain,
injustice, religious indifference
and of all human miseries are found.

In the Book of Revelation
Jesus says that he is
at the door and knocks.
Obviously, the text refers
to his knocking from
the outside in order to enter,
but I think about the times
when Jesus knocks from within,
so that we will let him come out.
The self-referential Church keeps
Jesus Christ within herself,
thus preventing him to come out
and meet his people.

When the Church
is self-referential,
she inadvertently believes
she is the source of her own light,
thus ceasing to be
the mysterium lunae
*(the mystery of the moon
that reflects the light of the sun),*
projecting instead the evil
of worldliness which is the worst
evil that can befall the Church.

❦ Let us not deprive the Church
of her ministry of prayer
which allows her to be
invigorated by giving testimony
about a God who is Father,
Mother, Brother, Sister and Spirit,
Bread, Way, Companion
and Giver of Life.

❧ The Church cannot side
with those who only see confusion,
dangers and threats neither
with those who intend to cover
the variety and complexity
of situations with a coat
of worn out ideologies
or irresponsible condemnations.
The Church's aim is to confirm,
renew and revitalize the novelty
of the gospel rooted in our history,
from a personal and communitarian
encounter with Jesus who makes
us disciples and missionaries.

When the Church does not
come out of herself to evangelize
she becomes self-referential
and then gets sick.
There are two images of the Church:
the Church that evangelizes
and comes out of herself,
and the worldly Church that lives
within herself, of herself,
for herself, falling into a sterile,
theological narcissistic limbo.
This should shed light on the possible
changes and reforms which must
be done for the salvation of souls.

☙ Thinking of the next Pope,
he must be a man who,
from the contemplation
and adoration of Jesus Christ,
helps the Church to go out
to the existential peripheries
which will help her to become
a fruitful mother, revitalized
by the *"sweet and comforting
joy of evangelizing."*

❧ As a priest and a bishop
I must be at your service.
It is a duty which comes
from my heart:
I love it!
Bishops, be close to your priests
with affection and with your prayers,
so that they may always
be shepherds according
to the heart of God.

❧ To be a priest is totally different
from being a religious official.
It is painful to see
the metamorphosis from priest
to religious official taking place little
by little in many ordained ministers.
Then the priesthood ceases to be
the bridge, *"the pontiff,"*
and ends up as a mere function
to be fulfilled.

❧ *How I would like
a Church poor
and for the poor!*

❧ I see the faults of the Church
as I see the faults and
shortcomings of my mother:
with understanding and love.
But when I think of her,
I remember the good
and beautiful things she did
and continues doing for me,
more than her weaknesses and defects.
I wonder whether there is any love for
the Church in the hearts of those who
pay so much attention to the scandals.
Let us not lose sight, then,
of the many holy men and women
who *"are"* the Church as well
as those who scandalize and sin.

≈ I must not be
scandalized by the fact
that the Church is my mother.
When we lose our identity as sons
or daughters, brothers or sisters,
members of the people of God,
we spend time in cultivating
an artificial, elitist
"pseudo-spirituality,"
thus leaving the fresh, green pastures
for the paralyzing sophisms of
a *"test-tube Christianity."*
We are no longer Christians,
but an *"enlightened elite"* with a
mere Christian burnish.

Church | 203

As Bishop of Rome
I would like to give the blessing,
but first I want to ask you a favor:
pray to the Lord to bless me
and say the prayer of the people
for their Bishop, then,
I will bless you.

The bishop's fidelity
to the gospel and his love
for the spirit of poverty
lead him to a special option
for the poor
who are at the central core
of the Good News of Jesus.
The bishop should
walk with them.

&✺ The priest
does not belong to himself.
He can sometimes take refuge
in other things,
but all these *"other things"*
should give preference
and get out of the way when,
for instance,
a mother of a family
asks him to walk several blocks
to bless her home.

I think that
the hands of a priest, rather
than expressing routine gestures,
must tremble with excitement
when administering baptism
or giving the absolution of sins
or blessing the sick because
they become instruments
of the creative power of God.

≈ In our ecclesiastical circumscription there are priests who do not baptize the children of single mothers because they were not conceived in the sanctity of marriage. These are the hypocrites of today, the ones who *"clericalize"* the Church and prevent God's people the access to the source of salvation.

❧ Vanity and boasting
smell of worldliness
which is the worst sin
the Church
can commit.

&❧ *"Clericalization"* is a problem in the Church. Priests *"clericalize"* the laity and the laity begs to be *"clericalized"* by the priests. *And to think that baptism alone could suffice!* I'm thinking of those Christian communities in Japan that remained without any priest for more than two hundred years. When the missionaries returned, they found them all baptized, all validly married and their dead properly buried with Catholic funeral. The faith had remained intact by God's grace which had gladdened the life of those lay men and women who had received only baptism and lived their apostolic mission in virtue of baptism alone. One must not be afraid of depending only on God's tenderness.

≈§ Nowadays the war of
the powerful against the weak
has created an abyss between the rich
and the poor. The poor are legions.
The present unjust economic
system with such strong structural
inequalities has worsened
the situation of the marginalized.
Today substantial groups of people
suffer hunger. The poor, the young
and the refugees are victims of this
"new order." Women in many places
are looked down upon and are the
objects of a new hedonist culture.
Bishops must never tire of preaching
the social teaching which comes from
the gospel and which the Church
has made explicit since the times
of the early Fathers.

Church | 211

🍃 How many times in my pastoral
ministry have I heard,
"Father, I have many sins,"
and how many times
have I always replied,
"Don't be afraid, go to him;
he is waiting for you,
he will take care of everything."

&9 Someone may think:
my sin is so great,
I am as far from God
like the younger son in the parable;
my unbelief is like that of Thomas;
I don't have the courage to go back;
it is hard to believe that God
can welcome me and more so that
he might be waiting for me.
But God is really waiting for you.
He only asks of you the courage
to go to him and say,
"Lord, I am here, accept my poverty,
hide my sin in your wounds
and wash it away with your blood."

JULY

"O God, be merciful to me, a sinner."
Luke 18:13

Mercy

🪶 If our heart is closed,
if our heart is made of stone,
then the stones will end up
in our hands and, then,
we will be ready to
throw them at someone.

🔖 *How beautiful is this gaze of Jesus, how much tenderness is in there! Brothers and sisters let us never lose trust in the patience and mercy of God!*

🖋 Let ourselves be embraced
by the mercy of God;
let us trust in his patience
which always gives us more time.
Let us find the courage
to return to his house,
to dwell in his loving wounds,
letting ourselves
be loved by him.
We will feel his tenderness
and we too will become
more capable of mercy,
patience, and forgiveness.

🔖 This is important:
let us have the courage
to trust in Jesus' mercy,
to trust in his patience
and to seek refuge always
in the wounds of his love.

God's face is that
of a merciful Father/Mother
who is always patient.
A little bit of mercy will make
the world less cold
and more just.

*❧ Have you thought
about God's patience?
The patience he has
with each of us?
That is Mercy!*

🐟 I have so often seen in my own
life God's merciful countenance
and his patience in action.
I have also seen so many people who
find the courage to enter
the wounds of Jesus by saying to him,
"Lord, I am here, accept my poverty,
hide my sin in your wounds
and wash it away with your blood."
And I always see that
God does just this:
He welcomes, consoles,
cleanses and loves
everyone coming to him.

Jesus has this message for us: mercy!

Our God
is so eager to forgive
that at the slightest sign
of repentance he is ready
with his mercy.
He does not forget
the covenant he made
with our ancestors.

Temptations

🦋 Ideologues falsify the gospel.
Every ideological interpretation,
wherever it comes from,
is a falsification of the gospel.
We have seen in the history
of the Church these ideologues
end up as being intellectuals
without talent, ethicists
without goodness,
not to speak about
beauty of which
they understand nothing.

༝ Never allow the evil spirit
to spoil the work you
have been called to do.
This evil spirit has very concrete
manifestations easy to detect:
anger, ill treatment,
close-mindedness, contempt,
negativity, routine,
murmuring, gossip.

🍎 Many men and women
are experiencing more
and more today serious lowliness
and neglect as a result
of their excessive zeal for autonomy
which they inherited from modernity.
But mostly they have
lost the support of something
that transcends them.

Let's get out of virtual realities and the cult of appearances.

🏺 It seems that *"public spaces"*
today must be *"sheltered*
from any conviction
or manifestation of religiosity,
even to the point of avoiding
at all cost the word 'God'."
Only vagueness and frivolity
have the right to be there
or those issues and matters
that fit the interests
of mass media owners.

🐚 *Is it not about time*
we realize that the worst thing
that can happen to us is not
to dream dreams and have hopes
to be developed and sustained,
but to stay in deathly shallowness
where nothing is relevant,
nothing has transcendence,
and to remain in this
lovey-dovey sort of culture?

🔊 May the *"today"* of Jesus
delete the *"past"* to which
often times we want to go back to
because of the present difficulties
or mere convenience,
and delete as well the kind
of future we try sometimes
to control because of ambition
or fear. *May Jesus firmly place us
in the "today" of God's love!*

⅏ As at the ethical level,
the right approach to others
is to help, not to hurt them.
At the level of truth, the right thing
to do regarding others is to provide
them with truthful information.
On an aesthetic level, to convey this
information in its integrity,
harmoniously and with clarity.
The wrong approach in conveying
information to others is to do it
with a disintegrating aesthetic,
hiding some aspects
of the problem or, what is worst,
manipulating the information
in order to create disharmony
that obscures reality,
disfigures it and denigrates it.

🕭 There is a permanent temptation
for the Church:
to put aside the cross
(cf. Mt 16:22),
to negotiate with the truth,
to avoid persecution,
thus diminishing
the redemptive power
of the cross of Christ.

❦ Sin can be forgiven
but not corruption,
simply because at the root
of every corrupt attitude
there is a fatigue for transcendence.
In front of God who does not
get tired of forgiving,
the corrupt person gets tired
of asking for forgiveness.

🔊 Murmuring
damages the spirit
of ecclesial unity.
St. Augustine describes
it very realistically:
"there are persons who recklessly
judge others, who are detractors,
gossipers, murmuring creatures;
who insist on suspecting
what is not seen or trumpeting
what they not even suspect."

❧ We must not believe
the Evil One when telling us
that there is nothing
we can do
in the face of violence,
injustice and sin.

🐟 It is not lawful to become
"untrustworthy" a priori
*(which is not the same as having
a critical mind)*
and congratulate ourselves
in our closed world
for our doctrinal clarity
and our incorruptible
defense of truths.
This utterly, uncompromising,
defensive attitude only ends up
serving our own pride.

Temptation
has its own *"style"*
in the Church:
it grows, spreads
and justifies itself.
It grows inside the person,
rising in tone.
It grows in the community,
spreading the disease.
It always has a word
at hand to justify its stance.

The crux of temptation
is faithful-unfaithfulness.
God, our Lord,
wants a loyalty that
is renewed at every test.
But there comes the devil,
the seducer.

🕉 Any triumphalism
hides the possession
of a worshipped idol.
The God of memory
has been transformed
into the memory
of a god made by us.

Violence

❧ Only God knows
how much violence
has been unleashed
in recent history by the attempts
to eliminate Him from
the horizon of humanity.
The need therefore to witness
in our societies the original openness
to transcendence that is inherent
in the human heart
is the top priority
of the mission of the Church.

> Let us not forget
> that hatred,
> envy and pride
> defile our lives!

Only from a personal encounter
with the Lord can we carry out
the *diakonia* (service)
of tenderness without letting us
get discouraged
or be overwhelmed
by the presence
of pain and suffering.

Everyone is unique
and uniquely important.
We should, therefore,
care for each person
and not allow a single violation
of the dignity of a woman
or a man be justified
in the name of any idea
or reason whatsoever.

We get used
to getting up every day
as if it could not be otherwise;
we become accustomed
to see violence in the news
as something inevitable;
we get used to the usual
landscape of poverty and misery
while walking the streets
of our city.

&. At the door
of our schools
death is sold (drugs).
The rule of money with
its demonic effects
as drugs and human trafficking
are commonplace.

AUGUST

"Jesus said to his disciples,
'When you pray, say this:
Father, may your name be held holy,
may your kingdom come;
give us each day, the kind of bread
we need, and forgive us our sins;
for we also forgive all who do us wrong;
and do not bring us to the test.'"
Luke 11:4

Prayer

❧ Be close to your priests
with affection
and with your prayers
so that they may always
be shepherds according
to God's heart.

🙠 The encounter with Jesus Christ
happens in daily life,
in one's personal search in prayer,
in the wise reading of the signs
of the times
(Mt 24:32; Lk 21:29),
and in the midst of
our brothers and sisters
(Mt 25:31-46; Lk 10:25-37).

Let us always pray
for one another.
Let us pray
for the whole world
that there may be
a great spirit
of communion.

Only in the contemplation
of the mystery of love
which goes beyond distances
and creates closeness,
will we find the strength
not to fall into the temptation
of stopping along the way.

"Only the Lord
will you worship!"
It is the only great unshakable rock
from which to confront
so many alluring invitations from
the evil ones which in reality
bring us only void and emptiness.
Do not worship contemporary idols
nor listen to their siren's
enchanting songs.
It is the great challenge
of our present day
for us believers.

To worship is to be filled
with the love we have for the one
with whom we enter into communion.
None of us worship anyone we don't
love or who doesn't love us.
We are loved by God!
We are dear to Him!
"God is love"!
This certainty is what leads us
to worship God with all our heart,
because *"He first loved us"*
(1 Jn 4:10).

≫ When Jesus encourages us
to pray with insistence
he sends us to the very heart
of the Trinity where, through
his holy humanity, he leads us
to the Father and promises
the Holy Spirit.

Prayer will lead the way
both in good and difficult times
to recognize the Word
in all the suffering flesh
as well as surrender
our flesh to the will of God
in order to live
according to the Spirit.

The prayerful persons
are doubly seduced,
by God and by people.
On the one hand, they cannot
do without God because
they need to constantly look for Him
as they know that they are beloved
and wanted by Him, nor can
they do without the people because
they feel the need to serve them
as they see in them the face of God.
The prophet Jeremiah felt
this experience to the core.

It isn't God who
must change but the person.
This is the obvious goal of prayer,
and that is the reason why prayer
is the privileged place of exile
where the revelation is given, that is,
the passage from what one thinks
of God to what he truly is.
It is an exodus of purification
where we are led by God through
the dark night of the exile on the way
to the contemplation of his face.
Then, we finally will be
changed and transformed
into the likeness of Him.

～ The intercessor
is a worshipper
who has understood
the deepest feelings of God
and clings to them,
despite contrary appearances.

 In prayer, our flesh,
identified with the Word
made flesh and moved by the Spirit,
longs for the Father.
This is the mystery that unfolds
in prayer and that promises us
a unique communion with the Father,
in the Spirit and through the Son.
He takes our flesh
and we receive his Spirit.

The prayer of praise
is born only in those who know
how to see in our history
the presence of a God
who works wonders.

Love

$ *Only those who serve*
with love
are able
to protect!

✢ We hear of many offers
from the world around us,
but let us take up
God's offer instead:
He himself,
a caress of love.

Love

✝ *Let us not forget that hatred,*
envy and pride defile our lives!
To be protectors, then,
also means to keep watch over
our emotions, our heart,
because they are the seat of good
and evil intentions
which can build up or tear down.

✝ It is in the wounds of Jesus
where we are truly secure;
there we encounter
the boundless love
of His heart.

✤ Only the simple appeal
of the commandment
of love - constant,
humble and unpretentious,
free of vanity
but firm in its conviction
and dedication to others -
can save us.

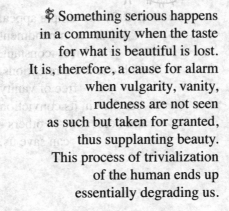

✻ Something serious happens
in a community when the taste
for what is beautiful is lost.
It is, therefore, a cause for alarm
when vulgarity, vanity,
rudeness are not seen
as such but taken for granted,
thus supplanting beauty.
This process of trivialization
of the human ends up
essentially degrading us.

✝ Lack of discipline
turns a priest into
an indiscreet individual,
and indiscretion is always
a lack of love.
Discreet love will help us
grow into the
*"full awareness of belonging
to a great community
which neither space
nor time can limit"*
(*Evangelii Nuntiandi* 61).

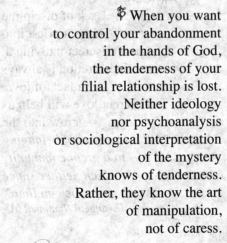

When you want
to control your abandonment
in the hands of God,
the tenderness of your
filial relationship is lost.
Neither ideology
nor psychoanalysis
or sociological interpretation
of the mystery
knows of tenderness.
Rather, they know the art
of manipulation,
not of caress.

✝ The power of love
is a service that resurrects
what is destroyed,
no matter how much it is so.
Its unattainable
and unquestionable source
is God's loving
fatherhood/motherhood.

✤ Love dispels ideologies.

✝ Tenderness
is not a virtue of the weak;
on the contrary,
it spells fortitude,
attentiveness, compassion,
openness to the other,
in short,
tenderness
is the daughter
of love.

✝ This is important:
the courage to trust
in Jesus' mercy,
in his patience,
to seek refuge
always in the wounds
of his love.

✣ We must not be afraid
of goodness,
even of tenderness!

✝ *For God we are not numbers!*
We are important;
indeed, the most important
of all his creatures,
the closest to his heart
whether we are saints
or sinners.

Ecology

§ In the end,
everything has been entrusted
to our protection
and all of us are responsible for it.
*Be protectors
of God's gifts!*

❦ Let us protect Christ in our lives
so that we might protect creation,
and, most important,
protect others,
especially those
who are less fortunate,
weak and suffering.
To protect means
to promote justice,
reconciliation,
to build peace
and respect the integrity
of creation.

We feel the closeness
also of those men and women who,
while not belonging to
any religious tradition,
feel however the need to search
for the truth, the goodness
and the beauty of God,
and who are our precious allies
in our efforts to defend the dignity
of human beings,
in building a peaceful
coexistence among peoples
and a careful protection
of creation.

§ Whenever human beings
fail to live up to this responsibility,
whenever we fail
to care for creation
and for our brothers and sisters,
the way is open
to the hardening of hearts
and the destruction
of our planet.

Ecology | 281

September

*"All the people were astonished
by Jesus teaching."*
Mark 11:18

Education

❦ Our goal is not
to form islands of peace
in the midst of
a disintegrated society
but to educate people
with the ability to
transform this society.
Therefore,
"fruits and results."

Every man and every woman have
the right to educate their children
in their religious values.
When a government deprives
children of this formation
it can lead to cases like Nazism,
when children were indoctrinated
with values alien to those held
by their parents.
Totalitarianism tends
to take over education
to feather its own nest.

🌱 If our schools
do not create another way
of being human, another culture
and another society,
we lose our time.
It is better to have free
and responsible learners,
capable of asking themselves
questions, to decide at the risk
of making mistakes rather than to
produce mere replicas of our
own successes
or our own errors.

Education | 285

Our educational work
should have a purpose:
to elicit a change in our students,
to make them grow in wisdom,
to help them undergo a transformation,
to provide them with knowledge,
with new feelings and,
at the same time, achievable ideals.
Many institutions promote
the formation of wolves
than of brothers and sisters
by educating their students
to compete and succeed
at the expense of others,
with only a few weak
ethical standards.

When we think of someone
like Mother Teresa of Calcutta,
our heart is filled
with a beauty that glows
from her charity
to the poorest
of the poor.

*May intolerance
and exclusion
never have a place
in our hearts,
in our words,
in our institutions,
in our classrooms!*

🔖 Three things are necessary
to educate in hope:
memory of the heritage
received and assumed,
work with this heritage
so that it may not become
a buried talent,
and vision through utopias
and dreams into the future.

🔖 *How many times do we close
the roads for renewal and growth
of a person or of an educational
institution by meekly declaring
"that is the way things are",
"that's the way they work"
or "with that person
there is nothing else to do"?*
Closed discourses always
conceal many delusions.
What is truly definitive
is not of this world.
We think of a school that is open
to new things, able to surprise
and ready to learn from
everything and everyone.

🎕 Let us dare to play entirely
by the Christian values
of fraternal solidarity.
Let us not allow the individualistic
and competitive mentality
so ingrained in our civic culture
to end up colonizing also our schools.
From our schools let us fight all forms
of discrimination and prejudice,
especially against the poor
and indigent foreigners,
and let this be manifested
in every decision, in every word,
and in every project.
Thus, we will be putting a very
clear sign, even a controversial
and contentious one if necessary,
of the different society
we want to create.

Education | 291

❧ Never will we be able
to show a student the horizon
of greatness if we use
our leadership as a stepping-stone
for our personal ambitions
or for our petty interests.
If we let our kids see in us
this counter-witness,
we make them afraid
to dream and grow.

CEREZO BARREDO 94

Communication

It is said that we are *"children of information and orphans of communication."*
Dialogue requires patience, clarity and good disposition towards the other.
It does not exclude the confrontation of different points of view, not as weapons but as beacons of light.
Let us not give up our ideas, utopias, convictions or rights but only the claim that ours are unique or absolute.

The mass media today is a major instrument in the creation of culture. Thanks to the media, communication reaches an immense audience. I like to categorize this power of the media according to the concept of *"fellowship."* Its strength lies in its ability to approach and influence the lives of people with a common global and simultaneous language. *Can one give simultaneously a gospel message that is not only highly customized but also "global"? How can we show love through mass media?*

Communication | 295

   Goodness,
truth and beauty
are inseparable
when we communicate.
Inseparable by their presence
or inseparable by their absence,
in which case
good will not be good,
truth will not be truth
and beauty will not be beauty.

✍ The media, unfortunately,
can mirror the society in its worst,
frivolous and narcissistic aspects.
But it can also be an open window
through which the beauty
of the love of God flows
gently and vibrantly
in the wonder of his works,
in the acceptance of his mercy,
and in solidarity and justice
with fellow humans.

Communication

ℒ The publication of some truths
can generate reactions
and often not only minor conflicts,
but the good communicator
does not act to generate
such conflicts or reactions
but to be faithful
to his/her vocation
and conscience.

❧ The communicator of partial truth
who chooses to do so does not build.
It is not necessary to deviate
from the truth to highlight
what is good in people.
Even in the most difficult
and painful situations
there is something good.
The truth is kind
and drives us
toward the good.

Communication | 299

The journalist who looks
for the truth also looks
for what is good.
Such is the union
between truth and goodness
that we can affirm
that a truth
which is not kind
is not true goodness.

✑ Truth and goodness
are always accompanied by beauty.
There is nothing
more touchingly human
than the need for beauty
for which the human heart longs.
Communication is more human
when it is more beautiful.

Communication | 301

A good communicator
is sensitive to beauty,
perceives it and does not
confuse what is beautiful
with what is fashionable
or only *"nice"*
or simply *"neat."*
Because it is human,
sometimes beauty is tragic,
amazing, touching;
it sometimes pushes us
to think what we do not want
or unmasks our errors.

ℕ The great challenge
of communicators,
searching every day
for the truth in order to tell it
to their listeners,
is to always remember
and realize that truth,
goodness and beauty
are inseparable.

To approach someone
in goodwill is to help
and not to hurt,
so information done
in goodwill includes
truthfulness,
integrity
and clarity.

  Happy are we
if we defend the truth
in which we believe,
even at the cost of being
slandered by the mercenaries
of propaganda
and disinformation.

Fortitude

§ Human history, that is,
our history, the history of each of us,
of our families, of our communities,
the concrete history we build
each day in our schools
is never *"completed"*,
never exhausts its possibilities.
On the contrary, it is always open
to what is new, to what has not been
taken into account until now.
Though it may seem impossible,
definitely it is not so, because
the horizon of new possibilities
is rooted in the creative
power and love of God.

§ We know that the enthusiasm,
the fervor with which we answer
the Lord's call cannot be the result
of an impulse of our own will.
It is a grace, an interior renewal,
a profound transformation
originating from a Presence
transforming our fears into fervor,
our sadness into joy,
our confinement
into new open horizons.

§ People who are afraid
will never make great progress
in virtue or carry out anything big;
the presumptuous person
will not persevere unto the end.
Both attitudes;
of courage and constancy
(*parrhesía* and *hypomoné* in Greek)
go together;
one implies the other.

Peace

> ॐ *There is no peace*
> *without truth!*

🦋 The heart is like a home.
There are houses that are open
because they are at peace;
they are welcoming
because they have warmth.
They are *"not so tidy"* as to make
people afraid even to sit down
neither so untidy as to become
an embarrassment.
The same goes for the heart:
the heart that has room for the Lord
also has space for others.

Women

God does not choose
according to human criteria.
The first witnesses of the birth
of Jesus were the shepherds,
simple and humble people,
and the first witnesses
of the resurrection
were women who,
driven by love,
knew how to accept
this proclamation
(of the resurrection) with faith.
They believed and immediately
they passed on the great news.

Women have a special role
in opening doors to the Lord,
in following him
and communicating his face
because the eyes of faith
always need the simple
but profound look of love.

This is the mission of mothers:
to give witness to their children
and grandchildren
that Christ has risen.
Faith is expressed with the lips
and with the heart,
with words and love.

Hope

"*Those who hope in the Lord
will renew their strength.
They will soar as with eagle's wings;
they will run and not grow weary;
they will walk and never tire.*"

Isaiah 40:31

❧ The only reason
for the importance
we give to the field of education
is the hope for a new humanity,
for another possible world.

To protect creation,
to protect every man
and every woman,
to look upon them
with tenderness and love
is to open up a horizon of hope;
it is to let a ray of light
break through the heavy clouds;
it is to bring the warmth
of hope!

We are in a time
of *"spiritual myopia
and moral shallowness"*
that try to impose
on us as normal
the *"culture of lowness,"*
where there is obviously
no place for transcendence
and hope.

Unity is kept
by taking care
of mediations.
And hope
is the mediator
par excellence
because it can bring
opposites together
through understanding
and mercy.

Hope | 321

Hope is not
a *"spiritual consolation,"*
a distraction from the serious tasks
that require our attention,
but a dynamic force liberating us
from all determinism
and every obstacle in order
to build a community
of men and women
finally free from the usual chains
of selfishness,
inaction and injustice.

To walk in hope
is to walk next to Jesus
in the darkest moments
of the cross when things
have no explanation
and we do not know
what is going
to happen next.

♒ *"Fear not,"*
the Angel said to Mary
in the announcement
of the incarnation of the Word.
"Do not be afraid,"
Jesus repeated so many times
to the disciples.
It is an invitation
that opens a new,
refreshing space in the soul,
giving security
and engendering hope.

❧ Let us follow Jesus,
knowing that he accompanies us
and carries us on his shoulders.
This is our joyful hope
that we must bring to this world.
*Please do not let yourselves
be robbed of the hope
that Jesus gives us!*

The spirit of sadness
is the most dangerous thief
and destroyer of hope.
How well Bernanos described it
in his *"Diary of a Country Priest"*!
The sin against hope
is the most deadly of all
but the most cherished,
nonetheless, for it carries within
itself a strange sweetness.
It is the most precious
elixir of the devil,
his most deceiving ambrosia.

❧ The pure hope in God
is given when,
as in the case of Jesus,
one gets to the bottom of failure,
when we are finally convinced
that there is no way out,
that everything is over,
that all doors are closed,
except the one of God.

For believers,
for us Christians…
the hope that we bring
is set against the horizon of God,
which has opened up
before us in Christ.
It is a hope built on the rock,
which is God.

Poor

The Church has made
a preferential option
for the poor
and that will have
to lead us to know
and value the way
of living the gospel
according to
their way of life.

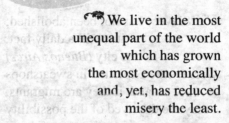

We live in the most
unequal part of the world
which has grown
the most economically
and, yet, has reduced
misery the least.

Slavery has not been abolished;
it is still a daily fact.
In this city *(Buenos Aires)*
workers are exploited in sweatshops
and, if they are migrants,
they are deprived of the possibility
of getting out of there.
In this city there are many children
living on the streets
who have been there for years.
This city has failed
and is failing to get rid
of that structural slavery
which exists in our midst.

The socio-economic crisis
and its resulting poverty
have its roots in policies
inspired by neo-liberalism
which considers earnings
and market laws
as absolute parameters
to the detriment of the dignity
of persons and peoples.

When we, as Church,
come to accompany the poor,
we see that beyond
the enormous difficulties
of their daily concerns,
they live with
a transcendent sense of life.
Somehow consumerism
has not yet engulfed them.

Jesus is the visible face
of the invisible God,
and the excluded
and marginalized of today
are the visible face of Jesus.
Contemplation
is the paradox
that allows the invisible faces
to become visible.

"*Life's*" destination lies beyond
this life because it depends on
"*Someone*" with a capital letter.
All this is rooted
in the hearts of our people,
even if they are unable
to express it conceptually.

In the same way,
there is also a beauty in the worker
who returns home dirty
and unkempt but with the joy
of earning the bread
for their children.
There is extraordinary beauty
in the communion of a family
at table and the bread shared
with generosity,
even if the table
is very poor.

Poor | 337

When the news
just makes us exclaim
"What a disaster!" and,
then, we turn the page
immediately or
change the channel,
we have destroyed
our *"fellowship,"*
we have further widened
the gap that separates us.

*How can there be people
who say that God does not speak,
that they don't understand
what God wants to say to us?*
It is clear: these people do not
listen to the poor,
the children, those in need.
They only pay attention
to the *"constant"* voices
of propaganda and statistics
and do not have ears to hear
what the simple folks are saying.

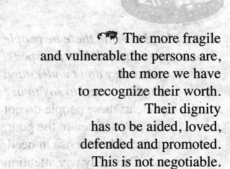

The more fragile
and vulnerable the persons are,
the more we have
to recognize their worth.
Their dignity
has to be aided, loved,
defended and promoted.
This is not negotiable.

If we choose to say *"yes"*
to some and *"no"* to others,
we leave the door open for all
aberrations that will come afterward.
We need to look again, to see that
no one is left out, no one forgotten.
And all these, for many reasons;
first, because in Christian logic
every person has his/her own place
and everyone is indispensable.
Second, because an exclusionary
society is, in fact, a potential
enemy of everyone and,
third, because the one
who was forgotten
will not give up so easily.
If you are not allowed to enter
through the door, you will try
to do it through the window.

There are many girls
in the slums,
who quit playing
with dolls
to enter a brothel.

Let us learn to look upward,
towards God and also downward,
towards others especially
the last ones.
And we must not be afraid
of sacrifice.
Think of a mom or a dad:
How many sacrifices!
But why do they make them?
For love!
And how do they face them?
With joy!
Because it is for the
people they love.
The cross of Christ,
embraced with love,
does not lead to sadness
but to happiness.

Justice

✐ Not only terrorism,
repression or assassination,
but also unfair economic structures
that create huge inequalities,
violate human rights.
In our cities
human sacrifice
takes place when the dignity
of men and women,
girls and boys are trampled upon
and they are reduced to slavery
by unjust economic systems.
We cannot remain silent.

Justice | 345

Report sex trafficking
which is the breeding ground
for slavery and the evil altar
where human sacrifices
are offered.
If we remain silent
we are accomplices
in this slavery.

We all,
teachers, principals,
pastors, parents, pupils,
can be signs of a different world
where everyone is recognized,
accepted, included, dignified,
and not only for their usefulness
but for their intrinsic value
as a human being,
as daughter or son of God.

The unjust distribution
of goods persists,
creating a situation
of social sin
that cries out to heaven
and limits the possibilities
for a fuller life
for so many
of our brothers
and sisters.

The realization
of social justice
challenges
the whole of society,
particularly the state,
the political leadership,
the financial capital,
entrepreneurs, agricultural
and industrial institutions,
trade unions, churches
and other social organizations.

Justice | 349

Human rights
are violated
not only
by terrorism
and repression
but also
by misery
and poverty.

NOVEMBER

CEREZO BARRETO 99

"Jesus said: 'do not be troubled!
Trust in God and trust in me!'"

John 14:1

Faith

Faith cannot be negotiated;
it requires courageous witness.
To believe in the Lord
is to always enter
anew through the door of faith
that makes us
set out on a journey
and leave
our comfort zones.

When one does not enter
through the door of faith
the door closes,
and fear
and the evil spirit
"sour"
the Good News.

It is good to realize
that today,
more than ever,
the act of believing
must allow the joy
of faith
to shine through.

Someone who believes
is a recipient of that beatitude
that runs through the
whole gospel and resounds
throughout history
as expressed through
the lips of Elizabeth:
"Blessed is she who believed"
or directed to Thomas
by Jesus himself:
*"Blessed are those
who have not seen
and yet believe!"*

Faith is always a grace,
an unmerited gift of God.
God pours out his love
on us permanently
and that is what makes us
Christians.

🖋 Faith is our response
to God's love,
it is finding a safe
support in God,
it is entering into communion
with the mystery of a love
which surpasses us
and surrounds us.
God gives grace
abundantly to all,
but especially
to the poor.

Faith | 357

Faith always expresses
itself culturally.
Children learn it
from their parents,
their teachers,
their catechists,
their environments.
Faith is above all
a divine grace but also
a human act and,
therefore,
a cultural act.

The faith of our people
is a slap in the face of secularism.
That is why it can be said
that popular piety
is an active evangelizing force
that carries with it
an effective antidote
against the advance
of secularism.

Faith | 359

God loves us.
We should not be afraid
of loving him.
Faith is expressed
with the lips
and with the heart,
with words and with love.

Our faith is by itself
revolutionary and militant,
but it is not to be carried out
with the militancy of a fanatic.
It is a revolutionary project
of changing the world,
discerned and brought
about under the guidance
of the Spirit.

Since faith
is so revolutionary
it will continually
be tempted by the enemy,
obviously not to destroy it
but to weaken it,
making it inoperative
by preventing it to be
in contact with the Holy,
the Lord of
all faith and life.

One of the most serious
temptations that lead us to break
our contact with the Lord
is the feeling of defeat.
Facing a combative faith
by definition, the enemy
under the disguise of an angel
of light will sow the seeds
of pessimism.
No one can take up
any fight if, from the outset,
one does not fully trust in winning.
Those who begin without trust
have already lost half the battle.

God did not create
human understanding
to become a judge of all things.
It is a borrowed light,
a reflection.
Our understanding
is not the light of the world.
It is simply a flash
to illumine our faith
just one step at a time.

🌿 The mission of our mind
is to discover the seeds
of the Word within humanity.
And this is what we should ask for.
God will only save us if we so ask
him with the untiring persistence
of one in a hopeless situation.
To deny that the prayer of petition
is superior to other forms of prayer
is the most refined act of pride.
A faith that lacks certainty is like
a confession of weakness,
the weakness of the one who does
not believe that faith can
"move mountains"; in other words:
the weakness of inefficiency.
To be *"strong in faith"* is a confession of power, of God's power.
It is to know where and how
to beat the devil of defeatism.

Faith | 365

"*Go out to the whole world and proclaim the Good News to all creation.*"
Mark 16:15

✄ Mission springs
from the certainty of faith
that coexists with the thousand
questions of a pilgrim.
Faith is not a matter of ideology,
existential security,
but of an irreplaceable encounter
with a living person,
Jesus of Nazareth.

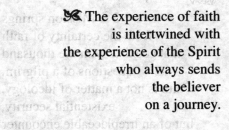

The experience of faith
is intertwined with
the experience of the Spirit
who always sends
the believer
on a journey.

Mission

❧ I ask you to see
your field of evangelization
as reaching beyond
those who are to be catechized,
thus you will spread the joy
and beauty of the faith
to their families
and friends as well.

❧ *"People,"*
is more than a word;
it is a calling,
a con-vocation to get out
of individualistic enclosures
and limited self-interests.
It is an immersion in the river
of history, of going forward,
gathering along the way
the experiences of others,
giving and receiving life.

Hopes and fears are intertwined even in our apostolic life, especially when important decisions are to be taken. To decide without taking into consideration our very fears and hopes is to run the risk of missing the point of *"Evangelii Nuntiandi"* that recommends that improvisation be avoided *"in times of uncertainty and discomfort where we must fulfill our ministry with growing love, zeal and joy."*

✭ Let us never forget that
authentic power is service,
and it goes as well for the Pope who,
in the exercise of his powers,
must enter ever more fully into
that service which has its radiant
culmination on the cross.
Only those who serve with love
are able to protect others.
The Pope must serve and protect
all people, especially the poor,
the sick, the vulnerable.

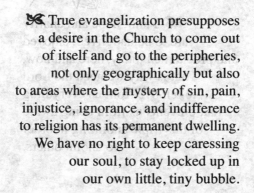

❧ True evangelization presupposes
a desire in the Church to come out
of itself and go to the peripheries,
not only geographically but also
to areas where the mystery of sin, pain,
injustice, ignorance, and indifference
to religion has its permanent dwelling.
We have no right to keep caressing
our soul, to stay locked up in
our own little, tiny bubble.

22 NOVEMBER

Faith, hope and charity
are to be had, lived, enjoyed
and proclaimed today, here and now.
That is why we need the Lord
to remove from us everything
that prevents us from being aware
of this triple anointing in order
to anoint others.

❧ *Poor and lukewarm*
is the Church that flees from
and avoids the cross!
She will become only
a "polite social" institution
in her sterility.
This is, ultimately, the price paid,
and indeed it is, by the people
of God for being ashamed
of the gospel and giving in
to the fear of giving witness.
If we do not confess Christ,
what then would we be?

Mission | 375

❧ We need to *"go out,"*
then, in order to experience
our own faith, hope and charity,
bringing their power
and redemptive efficacy
to the *"outskirts,"*
where there is suffering
and bloodshed,
where blindness longs for sight,
and where prisoners
are held in thrall
by so many evil masters.

❦ The mission necessarily puts us
in contact with the cross of Christ.
This is the sign that the
mission is in accordance
with the Spirit of God.
It is only by *"dying"* to everything
else that we understand what
we are asked to do and thus discover
the right ways to do it.
*"I can assure you that if the grain
of wheat that falls to the ground
does not die, it remains alone;
but if it dies it gives much fruit"*
(Jn 12:24).

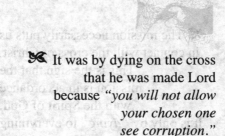

❦ It was by dying on the cross
that he was made Lord
because *"you will not allow
your chosen one
see corruption."*

🌿 *Go out into the streets
to look, find, knock on doors,
instruct and evangelize!*
In a history marked
by vulnerability our Lord
Jesus Christ breaks in with
an unstoppable
strength and courage.
That's the Good News,
the core of our preaching:
the outright proclamation
of this irruption of Jesus Christ
incarnate, dead and risen,
in our history.

Mission | 379

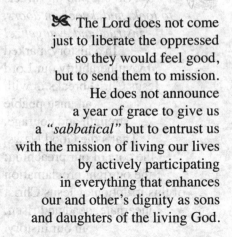

❧ The Lord does not come
just to liberate the oppressed
so they would feel good,
but to send them to mission.
He does not announce
a year of grace to give us
a *"sabbatical"* but to entrust us
with the mission of living our lives
by actively participating
in everything that enhances
our and other's dignity as sons
and daughters of the living God.

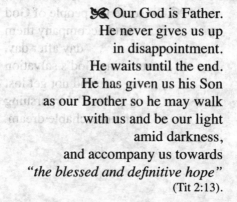

❧ Our God is Father.
He never gives us up
in disappointment.
He waits until the end.
He has given us his Son
as our Brother so he may walk
with us and be our light
amid darkness,
and accompany us towards
"the blessed and definitive hope"
(Tit 2:13).

❄ To serve the people of God
is to accompany them
day after day,
announcing God's salvation
and not get lost
in pursuing
an unreachable dream.

DECEMBER

God

"God so loved the world
that he gave his only Son
that whoever believes in him may
not be lost, but may have eternal life."
John 3:16

🕊 Christians don't believe
in an *"all-over-the-place"* god
like a *"god-spray,"* so to speak,
who is a little bit everywhere
but whom no one really knows
anything about.
We believe in persons
and when we talk to God
we talk to a Person.

God always waits for us, even when we have left him behind! He is never far from us, and if we return to him he is always ready to embrace us.

❧ God is always waiting for us;
he never grows tired.
Jesus shows us
this merciful patience of God
so that we can regain
confidence and hope…
always.

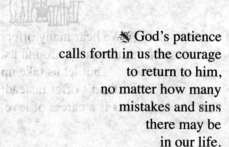

God's patience
calls forth in us the courage
to return to him,
no matter how many
mistakes and sins
there may be
in our life.

We hear many offers
from the world around us,
but let us take up
God's offer instead;
his is a caress of love.

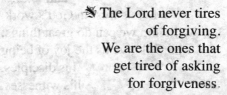

❧ The Lord never tires
of forgiving.
We are the ones that
get tired of asking
for forgiveness.

🦋 Let us trust in God's work.
With him we can do great things;
he will give us the joy of being
his disciples,
his witnesses.

🕊 God's love for us
is so great, so deep...
It is an unfailing love
always taking us
by the hand and supports us,
lifts us up
and leads us on.

🌿 We must keep alive
in our world the thirst
for the absolute
and not allow
the *"single-track vision,"*
which reduces the person
to what he/she produces
and consumes prevail.
This is one of the most
dangerous threats
of our time against life.

🕊 It is not possible
to build bridges
between people
while forgetting God.

❧ Let us allow ourselves
to be embraced
by the mercy of God;
let us trust in his patience
which always gives us more time.
Let us find the courage
to return home,
to dwell in his loving wounds.
Let us allow ourselves to be loved
by him and to encounter
his mercy in the sacraments.
We will feel his immensely beautiful
tenderness and embrace and, then,
we too will become more capable
of mercy, patience,
forgiveness and love.

❧ God is not impatient like us,
who often want everything at once,
even in our relationship with others.
God is patient with us
because he loves us
and so is able to understand,
hope, and inspire confidence.
Do not give up,
do not burn bridges,
be able to forgive.

🌿 To remember
what God has done
and continues doing for me,
for us, and to call to mind
the travelling we did together
is what opens our hearts
to hope for the future.

🌿 For God,
we are not numbers,
we are important,
indeed we are the most important
beings to him;
even if we are sinners
we are the closest
to his heart.

🦢 *How can we understand
that in some
educational environments
all topics and issues
are welcome for consideration
and discussion,
except one:* God?

From the economic point of view
  it is irrelevant to produce
  tanks or candies provided
  that the profit is the same.
Similarly, it might be the same
  to sell drugs or books
  if the figures match.
If the measure of value is money,
  everything goes provided
  that the profit does not vary.
The measure of every human being
  is God, not money.

God

When human time is no longer
tuned to God's time, it becomes
repetitive, boring, unbearable,
infinitely long or too short and,
what is worse, deadly *"times."*
Economic deadlines, for instance,
do not consider hunger or the lack
of schools for children or
the unhappy situation of the elderly.
Technology produces a kind of time
so instantaneous and full of images
that it does not let the hearts and
minds of young people mature.
Political time often seems
circular like a carousel
where the free-ring ride
is always taken
by the same people.

🌿 When we feel
the presence of God
in our daily lives,
we can only say
"God is here"
and the first thing to do
is to fall on our knees.

🕊 You can fool others
about the relationship
you have with God.
A pious posture,
a liturgy held with angelic face,
the breviary opened
and handy when someone enters
the room are masks
which have stuck so well
to certain persons
whom they really believed
to be respectable
and pious.

🍃 Sometimes I ask myself:
"To whom do you pray?"
And it is not hard to find the answer:
"To God", the Father or Jesus.
There also are many people
who pray to God as divine essence.
This is not prayer, of course.
Christian prayer is primarily
a person to person event;
we pray to the Father
or to the Son
or to the Holy Spirit.

God 403

Humanly speaking
we can say that
*"the heart of God is moved
by our intercession"*
but in reality he is always ahead
of us as he touches our heart
because he *"loves us first."*
What we make possible
with our intercession
is that his power, his love,
his loyalty and faithfulness
manifest themselves to us
with greater sharpness
and creativity.

❧ God does not want
a house built by people,
but faithfulness to his word
and acceptance of his design.
It is God himself
who builds the house
but of living stones
marked by his Spirit.

Joy

❧ *We are living out
the joy of walking with Jesus,
of being with Him,
of carrying his cross with love,
with a spirit that is
always young!*

❧ *The first word*
that I wish to say to you is joy!
Do not be sad people.
A Christian can never be sad!
Never give way
to discouragement!
Ours is a joy not born
from having many possessions,
but from having encountered
in our midst a Person:
Jesus who never leaves us alone
in difficult moments,
and is all the more present
when problems seem unbearable
and obstacles insurmountable.

❧ Our joy in God is missionary:
"We have found the Messiah"...
"He took him to where Jesus was"...
"Come and see"
(cf. Jn 1:41-46).

❧ With Jesus
we don't have to worry
about our death.
We are secure in the hands
of the One
who defeated death.

❧ Sadness
is the magic trick
of Satan
that hardens our heart
and embitters it.

❧ The joyful heart
always grows
in freedom.

The fundamental aspect of joy is that deep peace of the Spirit who is present in the most painful moments of the cross.

We are invited to ask the Holy Spirit for the gift of joy and jubilation. The contrary is sadness. Paul VI tells us that *"cold and darkness dwell in the heart of the person who is sad."*

As Jesus was filled with joy
in the Holy Spirit,
may our joy by the power
of the same Spirit
make us set our sight
on the things
of God's kingdom.

His Holiness
POPE FRANCIS

A PRAYER for POPE FRANCIS

O God,
shepherd and ruler of all the faithful,
look favorably on your servant Francis,
whom you have set at the head
of your Church
as her shepherd.

Grant, we pray,
that by word and example
he may be of service
to those over whom he presides
so that, together with the flock
entrusted to his care,
he may come to everlasting life.
Amen.